DK Life Stories

Anne
FRANK

Cathy & me to Barnes
Noble. + Tue. 3/12·19

DK Life Stories

Anne
FRANK

by Stephen Krensky

Illustrated by Charlotte Ager

Editor Allison Singer
Senior Designer Joanne Clark

Project Editor Roohi Sehgal
Additional Editorial Kritika Gupta
Project Art Editors Radhika Banerjee, Yamini Panwar
Jacket Coordinator Francesca Young
Jacket Designer Joanne Clark
DTP Designers Sachin Gupta, Vijay Kandwal
Picture Researcher Aditya Katyal
Illustrator Charlotte Ager
Pre-Producer Dragana Puvacic
Producer Basia Ossowska
Managing Editors Laura Gilbert, Monica Saigal
Deputy Managing Art Editor Ivy Sengupta
Managing Art Editor Diane Peyton Jones
Delhi Team Head Malavika Talukder
Creative Director Helen Senior
Publishing Director Sarah Larter

Subject Consultant Beth B. Cohen
Literacy Consultant Stephanie Laird

First American Edition, 2019
Published in the United States by DK Publishing
345 Hudson Street, New York, New York 10014

Copyright © 2019 Dorling Kindersley Limited
DK, a Division of Penguin Random House LLC
19 20 21 22 23 10 9 8 7 6 5 4 3 2 1
001–305912–Jan/19

A catalog record for this book is available from the Library of Congress.
ISBN: 978-1-4654-7543-5 (Paperback)
ISBN: 978-1-4654-7029-4 (Hardcover)

DK books are available at special discounts when purchased in bulk for sales promotions,
premiums, fund-raising, or educational use. For details, contact:
DK Publishing Special Markets,
345 Hudson Street, New York, New York 10014
SpecialSales@dk.com

Printed and bound in China

A WORLD OF IDEAS:
SEE ALL THERE IS TO KNOW

www.dk.com

Dear Reader,

Anne Frank. It was a simple name for a complicated girl, a young woman who has intrigued the world for four generations. Anne was a child caught up in a terrible war. She was forced into hiding, as were many others. She suffered for her heritage and religion, but again, so did many others.

So what sets Anne apart? Above all it is her diary, and that her funny, insightful, and honest writing reveals so much about both who she was and her vision of the world.

"Even though I'm only fourteen," Anne wrote, "I know what I want, I know who's right and who's wrong, I have my own opinions, ideas and principles . . ."

Anne was far from perfect. But that was okay because perfection wasn't really one of her goals. Anne wanted to be interesting, to captivate those around her. She did just that during her tragically shortened lifetime, and her story continues to do so today.

Stephen Krensky

The life of... Anne Frank

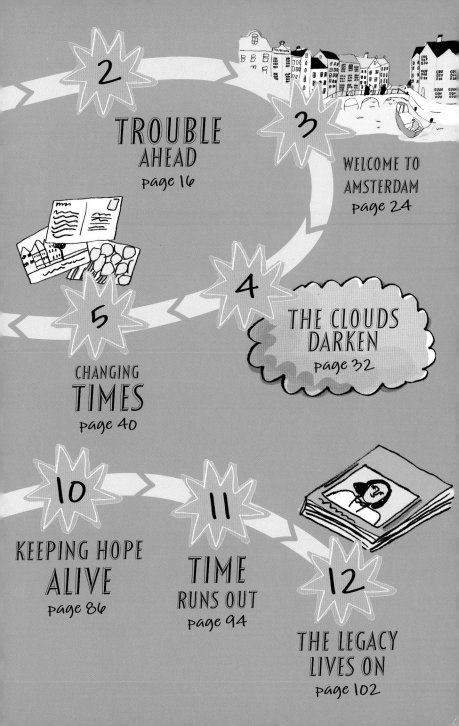

A noisy arrival

"I'll begin from the moment I got you, the moment I saw you lying on the table among my other birthday presents."

These were the first words that Anne Frank put in her diary on her thirteenth birthday. Much later the diary would become a famous book, read all around the world. For now, however, Anne was happy just to start writing in it.

Of course, the beginning of Anne's diary was not the beginning of her life. That moment had come thirteen years earlier, on June 12, 1929. Her parents, Otto and Edith Frank, were delighted to meet their new baby.

Their older daughter, three-year-old Margot, seemed pleased as well with her new role as a big sister. The baby's formal name was Annelies Marie Frank, but that was a bit of a mouthful, so she was known as Anne.

Otto and Edith thought they knew what to expect from a newborn because they had experience with Margot, who had been a joy from the beginning. As a baby, Margot had smiled a lot, taken regular naps, and almost never cried.

Anne, on the other hand, turned out to be more of a challenge. Maybe she was happy on the inside, but on the outside, she really didn't appear happy at all. Anne was a colicky baby, which is a nice way of saying that she cried a

lot. When she wasn't crying, she was nervous or fussy— or both.

What is colic?

A condition that can cause babies to cry for more than three hours without stopping. Most babies outgrow it after a few months.

Some babies soon sleep through the night, but Anne was not one of them, and it was Otto who most often comforted her in the hours before dawn. He was a devoted father who liked nothing more than to make up stories with his daughters. Edith did not play with the girls as much, but she made sure they were well cared for.

The Franks lived in the Marbachweg area of Frankfurt, Germany. They had lived there for several years while Otto struggled to save the failing family bank Anne's grandfather had founded.

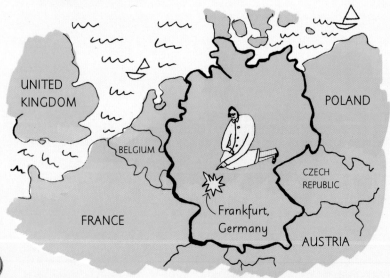

UNITED KINGDOM

POLAND

BELGIUM

CZECH REPUBLIC

FRANCE

Frankfurt, Germany

AUSTRIA

Otto poses for a picture with his two daughters, Margot and Anne, in 1931.

The Marbachweg neighborhood was welcoming. The children played together without caring about the differences between them, such as which families celebrated what holidays. The Franks were Jewish, but above all they considered themselves German, and they never thought about being only one or the other. They didn't have to.

Anne was still too young to do much playing with the older children, but she had grown into a lively toddler full of energy and charm. She could be stubborn, though, and would loudly complain if she didn't get her way. Margot was quite the opposite. She never got dirty because she knew she wasn't supposed to. Anne would happily plop down in a puddle and sit there, making a mess, until somebody made her get up.

DID YOU KNOW?

The Franks had several servants in their home when the girls were little, including a governess who helped care for Margot and Anne.

Anne and Margot were too young to understand the problems that their family and the rest of the world were facing.

13

Anne was born during a difficult time. Many countries were suffering.  There weren't enough jobs to go around, and everyday items were very expensive. In Germany, prices rose as inflation ran wild. The cost of bread could double in an hour. In a day or two, it could double again.

With money getting tighter, the Franks decided to move. In March 1931, they settled into a smaller apartment in what was called the Poets' Quarter. It was not as fancy as their old neighborhood, but it was a pretty area where the Franks soon felt at home. They hoped that, with luck, they wouldn't have to move again.

MONEY PROBLEMS

"Inflation" means an increase in prices. It occurs naturally over time—but when inflation is out of control, prices can soar. When prices get too high, people may not have enough money to buy the things they need to survive.

Inflation was high in Germany in the 1920s and early 1930s. Items cost so much money that paper bills were nearly worthless. Children sometimes used bundles of them as building blocks.

Chapter 2

Trouble ahead

Many countries were suffering because of a war that had ended in 1918, eleven years before Anne was born.

The generals in charge during the Great War, which would later be known as World War I, had begun their careers charging across battlefields on horseback. In the Great War, however, their weapons were upgraded to machine guns, tanks, and poison gas. Although their weapons had changed, their strategies and tactics had not. The result had been death and more death, a disaster for both sides in the conflict.

When the war was finally over, Germany was declared the loser. The country was ordered to pay heavily for the damage the war had caused. This was hard because the German people had suffered in the war, too. They did not have money to spare, but the war had to be paid for. The hard times that followed made the Germans sad, and it made them angry. Out of their extreme unhappiness, a new political party began to rise.

Otto Frank was drafted into the German army in 1915. He eventually rose to the rank of lieutenant.

The party's full name was the National-Socialist German Workers' Party, and its members became known across the world as the Nazis. The Nazis did not believe that the Germans were to blame for the war or for their hardships. Instead, they believed the blame lay elsewhere—especially with the Jews.

GAINING STRENGTH

In government elections in 1928, the Nazi Party won less than two percent of the popular vote, which means only two percent of Germans agreed with it. Four years later, it would become the strongest political party in the country.

Anti-Semitism was a popular sentiment in Germany (and in many other countries as well). When times were good, this feeling would often

Adolf Hitler

retreat into the shadows, but in bad times, it boldly stepped forward into the light. The Nazi Party leader, a former World War I corporal named Adolf Hitler, had written a book in 1925 called *Mein Kampf (My Struggle)*. In the book, he wrote about getting rid of the Jews. Even more ominously, he wrote that doing so would need to be "a bloody business."

As the Nazis led rallies through the streets, more and more Jews were attacked and injured. Anne and Margot were too little to understand what was happening, but their parents were not. At first Otto did not believe that a Jewish family like his, which was not very religious, could ever be a Nazi target. Surely that was not possible.

---

what is
anti-Semitism?

A hatred of all things Jewish, including Jews themselves.

Hitler arrives in Berlin, Germany, in the late 1920s and is greeted by a crowd of his supporters.

On January 30, 1933, Adolf Hitler became the chancellor, or leader, of Germany. Many German Jews continued to believe that the violence would lessen, and that it couldn't possibly get any worse. There were too many good people in Germany to let more terrible things happen.

And yet, they did. The Nazis made changes quickly, and these changes became more and more severe as their power grew. On April 1, the Nazis organized a national boycott of Jewish shops, Jewish lawyers, and Jewish doctors. German Jews kept hoping each new restriction would be the last.

WHY A BOYCOTT?

During a boycott, people refuse to deal with a person or company. They try to convince others to do the same. Their goal is to cut off the subject from its usual resources. By boycotting Jewish businesses, the Nazis made it hard for them to succeed.

This sign says "Germans! Protect yourselves! Do not buy from Jews!"

Fearing for their safety, the Franks left Frankfurt that summer. They moved in with Edith's mother in Aachen, Germany, a town near the Belgian border.

Anne loved spending time with her grandmother. She was also growing up, becoming someone who spoke her mind and was not easily intimidated. One time she and her grandmother were boarding a crowded streetcar, and Anne noticed there were no seats available. "Won't someone offer a seat to this old lady?" she is said to have shouted to the other passengers.

Aachen was 124 miles (200 km) from Frankfurt, Germany's largest city, but Otto knew they would not be safe there for long. He now realized they must leave Germany entirely. At the same time, Otto didn't fool himself into thinking their exile would be temporary. Looking back, he later wrote, "Though this did hurt me deeply, I realized that Germany was not the world, and I left my country forever."

Fortunately he knew where they would go, having spent some time working for the family business in Amsterdam, the Netherlands. It was the best place for a fresh start.

"I realized that Germany was not the world, and I left my country forever."

Otto Frank,
in a letter to a
friend in 1968

23

Chapter 3

WELCOME TO **Amsterdam**

When Anne looked back a few years later, she remembered the move to Amsterdam as a hectic time.

Anne's father had gone ahead to the Dutch city of Amsterdam in the summer of 1933, setting up a company that manufactured some of the ingredients in jam. Her mother followed

him there in September, while Anne and Margot stayed in Aachen with their grandmother. Margot went to Amsterdam in December and, Anne later recalled, "I followed in February [1934], when I was plunked down on the table as a birthday present for Margot."

Amsterdam was an old and beautiful city, filled with canals that helped keep the ocean from getting too close. At the time, the Netherlands had a Jewish population of about 100,000, many of whom lived in Amsterdam. Jews were more accepted there than they were in Germany.

Amsterdam, the capital city of the Netherlands, is known for its canals.

Anne, now four years old, and Margot, eight, started in the public school near their apartment. Their first challenge was to learn Dutch, the language of the Netherlands. Their father had begun before them, as he had already been living in Amsterdam, but the girls were quick learners and soon passed him by. Their mother, though, never stopped having trouble with a language she had little interest in and had never thought she would need to know.

On top of everything else, Edith worried about Anne's health. At different times, she had whooping cough, chicken pox, or the measles,

and her school records show she missed a lot of days—and even weeks at a time—with other ailments. One persistent fever seemed to come and go but never fully depart. No one was sure of the cause. Anne's parents took to calling her *Zartlein*, which means "fragile one." It was always said with affection, but with a strong dose of worry thrown in, too.

Neither the nickname nor the illnesses themselves seemed to bother Anne so much. Nobody wants to be sick, but Anne liked being spoiled and staying home from school. She enjoyed her own company and exercising her imagination.

When Anne was feeling better, she made friends, especially with other girls from families that had also relocated from Germany. Anne was shy around strangers one-on-one, but in a group she enjoyed being the center of attention. Miep Gies, who was then a young woman working for Otto, wrote that Anne "developed the skill of mimicry."

Miep Gies would become one of the Frank family's closest friends.

Miep added that Anne "would mimic anyone and anything, and very well at that: the cat's meow, her friend's voice, her teacher's authoritative tone. We couldn't help laughing at her little performances."

Anne also had one rather unusual skill. She could dislocate her shoulder on purpose—and then pop the shoulder right back into its joint. It was a rare, if not useful, ability, and the other children would laugh when she performed it for them. Though it was a popular trick at school, Anne's shoulder sometimes kept her on the sidelines during the rougher school sports.

Like many children her age, Anne collected pictures of movie stars and pinned them to her bedroom wall. She and her friends also liked to collect photographs of the Dutch and English royal families, whose lives they enjoyed

trying to imagine from far away.

Sometimes relatives would travel to visit the family in Amsterdam, including Otto's brother Herbert from Paris. Anne took to calling Herbert "Uncle Blue Dot" after she found a tiny birthmark on the side of his nose.

Otto was focused on making his business a success, but Edith still had hope that someday they would all be able to return home to Germany.

Princess Juliana and Queen Wilhelmina of the Netherlands were two of Anne's favorite royals.

This was a hope that made her feel better, even when there was no evidence to think it would ever come true.

In this picture of Anne's classroom in 1935, she is sitting in the back of the room, in front of the teacher. The Franks were lucky to find a school in Amsterdam where Anne and Margot were welcomed as new students, and where it didn't matter where they had come from or what religion they practiced.

4

THE clouds darken

In Amsterdam, Anne and her family were no longer in any immediate danger from the German government.

However, the Jews who were still in Germany were not so lucky. In August 1934, Hitler had become the head of both the government and the armed forces. He had the power to do anything he pleased. *Anything.* The country's laws meant nothing if they went against what he wanted. He would just create new laws of his own.

With alarming speed, Hitler and the Nazis put more and more restrictions on the Jews in their midst. The Nuremburg Laws of 1935 created a new set of rules for Jews in Germany. Jews could no longer marry other Germans or work in many professions. German women under the age of 45 could no longer work in Jewish households. Many Germans got caught up in ridding their culture of what they now saw as unacceptable elements. Because of this, books by Jewish authors were widely burned.

NUREMBURG LAWS OF 1935

The Nuremburg Laws were designed to take Nazi ideas and weave them into German laws. This provided a legal reason first for isolating Jews within German society, then persecuting them without mercy. The key element to the laws was that Jews were no longer considered to be of German blood, and therefore were no longer German citizens. With this rule as a base, any rights or privileges Jews had held in the past were stripped away. Their status crippled within German society, they could now be attacked in many ways with little to no chance of defending themselves.

A few months later, on November 9, 1938, Jews throughout Germany were attacked as never before. Homes and businesses were vandalized, windows were shattered everywhere, and many buildings were burned to the ground. This incident became known as *Kristallnacht*, which means the Night of Broken Glass.

On *Kristallnacht*, dozens of Jews were killed, and tens of thousands were sent off to prisons. Among the imprisoned Jews was Anne's uncle Walter, her mother's brother. Luckily he was later released and allowed to leave Germany.

In Amsterdam, Anne's daily life, whether she was at school or playing with her friends, was as normal as her parents could make it. They didn't want her or Margot worrying about the larger world and the terrible events beyond their control. For now Amsterdam remained a safe haven, but how long would this last?

A worker clears the broken glass from a shop after the riots of *Kristallnacht*.

Otto wanted to believe that the Germans would leave the Netherlands alone. But what if that was not true? What if the Franks were still in danger? Otto and Edith had no wish to uproot their daughters a second time. Both girls considered Amsterdam their home. Anne's thoughts of Germany were only a collection of dim memories.

Plus, even if they were in danger, there was no obvious place for them to go. Emigrating had become difficult. The Franks couldn't simply pick a destination and buy train or boat tickets. Special papers now had to be acquired and approved. They would need to prove they would not be a burden on whatever country would allow them in.

what is emigration?

The act of people moving permanently from one country to another. As tensions grew in the 1930s, many people emigrated from their homes to start new lives in other countries.

Such proof was hard
to come by. There was so
much paperwork and lots
of complicated procedures
for them to navigate. Otto
considered the possibility
of going to England or
America, but while he managed
to get some support for these ideas,
he was unable to get enough to make them
happen. He continued to work on growing his
business in the Netherlands, hoping that doing
so would somehow help the situation.

At the same time, everyday life went on.
Anne was growing up, but in many ways she
had not changed. She was still willful and
rebellious. She still insisted whenever possible
on getting her own way.

In May 1939, on his 50th birthday, Otto
wrote Anne a note. In the note, he told her,
"things haven't always gone as smoothly for
you as they did for your sister, though in
general your sense of humor and your

DID YOU KNOW?

About 85,000 Jews emigrated from Europe to the United States between March 1938 and September 1939.

amiability allow you to sail through so much so easily."

Anne treasured these kind words from her father. Her amiability, meaning her agreeable nature, and her sense of humor had served her well in the past, and she believed they would continue to do just that.

In 1939, some parents in Germany sent their children to England or America to avoid the war.

Jewish refugees (people who flee their country to find safety elsewhere) left Germany however they could, including by boat.

5

Changing times

Anne turned 10 on June 12, 1939. She celebrated the happy occasion by having a party with eight of her closest friends.

They played games and ate treats—and, as the guest of honor, Anne got to be the center of attention the whole time. She liked that.

Anne was an ordinary 10-year-old girl in many ways. She giggled and yelled and played and dreamed her way through school days and vacations. Anne could still picture herself becoming an actress in the future, and she still loved to follow the adventures of the royal families. The two young British princesses, Elizabeth and Margaret, were about her same age, so they became her most special concerns.

Anne thought of herself as having increasingly adult ideas about the world and how she would someday fit into it. In her own eyes, she was becoming quite grown up. Perhaps other people could not see this as clearly as she could, and they still treated her like a child—but she had no doubt most people would come around.

Margot and Anne on a beach in July 1939. The lady smiling in the background is their beloved grandmother.

Margot, however, was probably not one of them. Some sisters become great friends. They may share confidences and tell each other secrets. Anne and Margot were not so close. Margot continued to be an excellent student and was polite and well behaved. Anne, on the other hand, continued to be unpredictable and impulsive.

One thing they did share was thinking of Amsterdam as home and not merely a place of exile. But this home was now threatened, because there was a lot of bad news in Europe—and it all concerned the Nazis.

Hitler's dream of creating a German empire had come true. He had begun slowly, taking over the Rhineland in 1936 and then announcing the *Anschluss* (the merging of Germany with Austria) in 1938. Each of these was a bold move. It was as though Hitler was daring other countries to argue with him, but England and France, while looking on disapprovingly, were still suffering from the effects of World War I. They protested, but not loudly enough.

Hitler enters Braunau, Austria, in 1938.

So Hitler kept going. In March 1939, he took over Czechoslovakia. At last England and France tried to put their foot down. They insisted that the German expansion should go no further. If it did, that would mean war.

Hitler didn't seem to care. On September 1, 1939, the Germans marched into Poland. Two days later, Great Britain and France declared war on Germany.

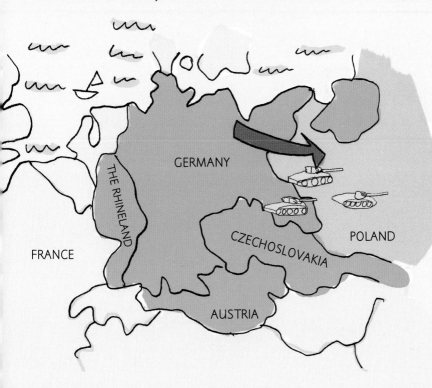

Germany's invasion of Poland in 1939 directly led to the start of World War II.

None of this was good news for the Frank family. Like most of their friends, they listened to news reports from London on the radio.  The Germans seemed to be winning on every front. Nobody could stop them.

At fourteen years old, Margot was mature enough to recognize the dangers that lay on the horizon. "We often listen to the radio as times are very exciting," Margot wrote to her pen pal, Betty, who lived in Iowa, "and being a small country we never feel safe."

---

what are pen pals?

Two people who write letters back and forth to each other. Pen pals have often never met in person.

Three years younger than Margot, Anne seemed less troubled, or at least she kept her worries to herself. She, too, had been writing to a pen pal—Betty's younger sister, Juanita.

Unlike Margot, Anne didn't seem anxious in her letters. Instead, she mentioned only everyday things, such as details about her family and her classes at school.

When ending a letter to Juanita on April 29, 1939, Anne referred to herself as "your Dutch friend." Any thoughts or feelings she had of being German or from Germany had apparently been left in the past.

There were some chances for Otto and Edith to send the girls to safety in England, but they could not bear to break up the family.

They refused to believe they were truly that desperate, and they clung to the hope that the Netherlands could sit out the war. After all, it had managed to stay on the sidelines in World War I.

But that time had passed. Hope faded as rumors of a German invasion kept popping up. Then one day the rumors became true. On May 10, 1940, German tanks and soldiers rolled into the Netherlands. Five days later, the Dutch, knowing they were hopelessly outmatched in strength, surrendered.

Here are the advancing
German armed forces.

German armed forces cross over a bridge and into the
Netherlands during the invasion on May 10, 1940.

German paratroopers invade
the Netherlands from the sky.

After the invasion, the Dutch city
of Rotterdam is left devastated.

Chapter 6

New worries

When they had lived in Germany, the Franks, like many Germans, had wrongly thought that the Nazi threat wouldn't last.

In Amsterdam, though, they knew better from the start. Over the next few months, the Nazis created a list of restrictions and guidelines that made their intentions perfectly clear.

Many of these rules concerned the Jews. They could not ride in cars or on bicycles, even ones they owned. They had to be inside after 8:00 p.m. (they couldn't even sit outside in their yards), which mattered less because they also could no longer attend a public concert, play, or movie. Public athletic facilities were now banned to them as well, and all Jewish-owned businesses had to be specially registered with the government.

Jews could no longer mix in with everyone else as they went about their lives. They had to identify themselves with a yellow-star patch sewn onto their coats.

Some Jews were allowed to stay in their homes and obey these restrictions. They were actually the lucky ones. Others were rounded up immediately for what was called a "voluntary relocation," but there was nothing voluntary, or optional, about it. The people who were forced to leave were not free to go where they pleased. They were directed to special camps that the Germans had recently constructed. For the moment, their futures were unknown.

DANGEROUS TRADITION

At different points in history dating all the way back to the 8th century, religious leaders have sometimes forced a certain group of people to wear badges to identify themselves. The Nazis adopted this tactic knowing it would help them identify and isolate the Jewish population of Europe.

Edith Frank liked to remind her girls to enjoy what they could, but there was increasingly less and less to enjoy at all. It was now very clear to Otto and Edith that their family was in grave danger. The threat might not come today or tomorrow, but it was surely coming.

Ironically given the uncertain times, Otto's business had improved enough by the end of 1940 that he had needed to move to larger quarters. The place he chose, at Prinsengracht 263, had a warehouse on the ground floor with offices on the two floors above. There was also an annex in the rear of the warehouse that could be reached only through a narrow hallway.

For Margot and Anne, the biggest change came the next September, when they were forced to change schools. Jews were no longer welcome at the school Margot and Anne had been attending for the past eight years.

Otto's staff stands in front of their old office. Miep Gies is on the far left.

Anne smiles for her school portrait at the Jewish Lyceum in Amsterdam.

This was not the school's choice—it was yet another restriction put in place by the Nazis. The girls now had to attend the Jewish Lyceum, a school designated for Jews alone.

It was unsettling to have to change schools, but Anne liked her new class. Her teachers were also Jewish, having been forced to relocate from other schools. They were devoted to their students and taught them well. If they were nervous about what further restrictions or hardships might lie ahead, they somehow managed to keep their focus on the present.

Anne was upbeat in a letter to her grandmother in Switzerland in the spring of 1942. "I'm still enjoying the lyceum," she wrote. "There are 12 girls and 18 boys in our class. At first we ran around with the boys a lot, but now we're not and it's a good thing, because they're getting too fresh."

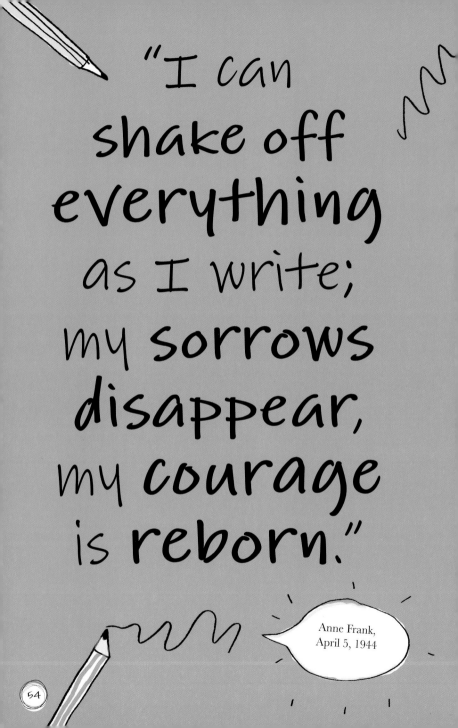

Best of all, Anne had a proper celebration for her 13th birthday in June. There was cake and presents, especially a notebook covered in red-and-green checkered cloth. The book closed with a small metal tongue that fit into a lock.

Some people would have used it as an autograph book. Others might have filled its pages with drawings. But Anne had a different purpose in mind, one that would help her forget her troubles and allow her imagination to soar.

For Anne, it was a diary.

Anne wrote this diary entry in 1942, the same year she had received the notebook. When Anne wrote in her diary, she was not trying to impress anyone. She was simply collecting her thoughts and memories, and trying to be as honest as possible. She saw her diary as a reflection of who she truly was.

Dit is een foto, zoals ik me zou wensen, altijd zo te zijn. Dan had ik nog wel een kans om naar Holywood te komen. Maar tegenwoordig zie ik er jammer genoeg meestal anders uit.

Annefrank.
10 Oct. 1942.
Zondag.

7

Disappearing act

One of the first things Anne mentioned in her diary was "a throng of admirers who can't keep their adoring eyes off me."

She may have been teasing herself a little about this, but clearly her spirits remained good despite the many restrictions that now hemmed in Jews on all sides.

Anne's everyday world was smaller after the German invasion, but in many ways it was still the world of a regular teenage girl. In her diary, Anne wrote about her friends, her teachers, and the extra homework assignments she had to do. One of the assignments was an essay about a chatterbox, which may have been her teacher's not-so-subtle way of telling Anne something about herself.

Then, suddenly, everything changed.

Anne stands on a sidewalk in Amsterdam in 1941.

On the afternoon of July 5, 1942, an official notification was delivered to the Frank home. Otto had assumed for some time that he might receive a summons ordering him to report to one place or another. There were rumors about what happened to those who obeyed these letters. Ending up in a labor camp was one possibility. There was also talk of concentration camps. Not as much was known about them, but people who went there were not expected to survive.

In this case, Otto was right about the summons, but wrong about whom it was for. Margot was the one being called up.

It didn't matter what the Germans were planning for Margot—Otto and Edith would never let her leave. But what should they do next? If they ignored the summons, German officials would come and take Margot away by force. They needed a different plan.

---

what is a summons?   An official request or command to appear at a specific place, usually at a chosen time.

CALLED TO THE CAMPS

Otto Frank had heard about the camps. They were terrible places where the Nazis imprisoned people from the countries they occupied during World War II. The purpose of a labor camp was to supply the Nazis with workers who would perform tasks without being paid. Death camps had a different objective: to kill their prisoners as efficiently as possible.

These gates at the front of a camp say "*Arbeit macht frei*," or "Work sets you free." This was a lie.

Anne had heard her parents mention the possibility of going into hiding, but that was all she knew. As she wrote, "where would we hide? In the city? In the country? In a house? In a shack? When, where, how . . . ?"

Otto and Edith had actually been preparing to leave for months. They had secretly moved furniture, bedding, dishes, and other goods to a special location. They had even settled on a date, July 16, for the move itself. But now that Margot had received a summons, waiting even one more day might be dangerous. They had to go at once.

They were not leaving the Netherlands. Spies and watchers were everywhere. Had they tried to do so, they would have soon been caught. But Amsterdam itself still gave them a chance. Whether it was a good chance or a bad chance didn't matter. It was simply the only chance that they had.

At the back of Otto's office and warehouse at Prinsengracht 263 was another building, an annex. It was bordered by other buildings on the sides and back. The only way to enter it was through Otto's offices, and even there, only one door and hallway linked the annex to the building in front. It was also hidden from the street by the buildings on either side. The annex could be seen from behind, but there was no particular reason to pay any attention to it.

This annex was the family's destination. On Monday morning, July 6, they left their apartment for the last time, leaving behind a note suggesting that they had gone to Switzerland. Anne also had to leave behind her cat, Moortje.

BELOVED CAT

Anne wrote in her diary that Moortje was the "only living creature I said goodbye to" before going into hiding. Later on, Anne wrote that she still missed her "every minute of the day."

As Anne wrote in her diary, it was too risky for any Jews to "leave the house with a suitcase full of clothes," so whatever they were going to bring, they had to wear. Anne herself had on "two undershirts, three pairs of underpants, a dress and over that a skirt, a jacket, a raincoat, two pairs of stockings, heavy shoes, a cap, a scarf and lots more."

Since Jews could not take public transportation, the Franks walked the distance to the office. If anyone had been looking closely, questions might have been asked. Fortunately nobody was, and the Franks arrived safely at the place they would now call home.

Viewed from the front, the building at Prinsengracht 263 looked like any other building in Amsterdam—but behind it hid the secret annex.

Chapter 8

Hidden life

The whole idea was simple enough. The Franks must stay hidden until the war was over. But when would that happen?

How long would the war last? For now the new German Empire covered most of Europe and spilled into North Africa. So much fighting on so many fronts would not be coming to an end anytime soon.

Therefore the Franks faced a daunting challenge. They were not tucked away in some remote country cabin. They were hiding in a few rooms in the middle of a bustling city. For their presence to remain a secret, they would have to be very careful. No noise could be made during the day that might alert workers in the offices below. Clearly that meant no talking, but there was more. It also meant moving around as little as possible. Just one creaky floorboard could give them away. Even a simple act like flushing the toilet would be dangerous. What if the workers heard water rushing through the pipes from above where no one was supposed to be?

Prinsengracht 263 (the annex)

AMSTERDAM

Houses lined the canals in this bustling city.

The Franks used to live southeast of here.

Even after the workers had gone home for the day, the Franks still had to be extremely cautious. No lights could be used at night without making sure the curtains had been tightly drawn. Otherwise nearby neighbors might get a little too curious.

While the Franks were willing to make sacrifices, they would not be able to survive on their own. Someone from the outside would need to take care of them—and in fact, this would not end up being just one person, but a small group of loyal friends willing to risk their own lives.

Johannes Kleiman and Victor Kugler, who were Otto's partners and helped him run the business, provided enough money for financial support. Miep Gies and Bep Voskuijl, two women who also worked for the company, helped by getting the Franks their food and seeing to their other everyday needs.

THE HELPERS

To the outside world, these people were simply doing their jobs and going about their everyday lives. Nobody suspected that they were secretly helping the Franks.

1. **Johannes Kleiman** was already a good friend of the Franks before Otto hired him as a bookkeeper in 1938.

2. **Victor Kugler** was a German World War I veteran like Otto who had then become a Dutch citizen in 1938.

3. Hermine **"Miep" Gies** met the Franks soon after they moved to Amsterdam in 1933 and became close to the whole family.

4. Elizabeth **"Bep" Voskuijl** was only 18 years old when Otto first hired her to work for him in 1937.

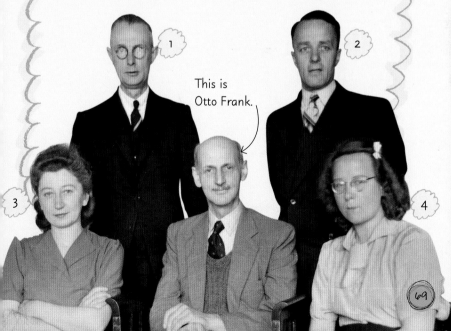

This is Otto Frank.

On the positive side, the annex was not a dark cellar or cramped attic, which was the more typical kind of hiding space. It had four rooms on two floors and an attic.

DID YOU KNOW?

The Franks called their hiding place *Achterhuis*, which translates into English as the "back house."

What did Anne think of all this? Well, unsurprisingly, she wasn't crazy about it. The idea of being with only her family all the time was hard to bear—but her parents had never actually intended for them to live there alone.

First floor	Second floor	Third floor

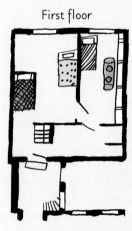 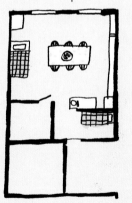 

Anne's bedroom was on the first floor of the hiding place. She often went to the third floor (the attic) to write in her diary, get fresh air from the window, and be alone with her thoughts.

A week after their arrival, Anne and her family were joined by the van Pels family: Hermann, a business partner of Otto's; his wife, Gusti; and their 16-year-old son, Peter. They, too, were Jewish and in danger from the Germans, and the Franks had planned for them to live in the annex as well.

The arrival of the van Pels family did make things a bit more crowded, however. The Franks slept in the two rooms on the first floor of the hiding space— above the street-level office—while the common room on the second floor of the hiding space became Hermann and Gusti's bedroom at night. Peter had a small room to himself.

Peter van Pels

Anne got to know the three van Pelses very well. Hermann was a man of many opinions, and he never hesitated to share them. Gusti did not always share his views, and she never hesitated to argue with him about them. As for Peter, he was much quieter than his parents. When he did speak, it was often to complain about one problem or another.

Anne could do without the complaining, but overall she liked the new arrangement. Though there was less space to call her own, she enjoyed having more people around. "From the first," she wrote, "we ate our meals together, and after three days it felt as if the seven of us had become one big family."

The van Pelses also brought news from the outside world, such as how the Frank family's disappearance had been received. Before they had gone into hiding, the Franks had taken care to leave behind clues that would throw the police off their trail—such as an address on a scrap of paper that suggested they had gone to Switzerland. Hermann had known the truth of their whereabouts, but when the police came to ask him about it, he added his own touch to

the false story: He pretended to remember
a high-ranking Swiss officer who had visited
Otto a few months earlier.

Anne and her family were pleased to hear
this news, and they were grateful for what
Hermann had done. It meant that if the Dutch
or German authorities decided to go hunting
for them, they would set off looking in the
wrong direction.

After a few weeks, one more change was added to their new home. Bep Voskuijl's father, Johannes Voskuijl, designed and built a bookcase that concealed the entrance to the annex. When the bookcase was closed, someone passing by would not even suspect the annex existed. The Franks hoped that this final touch would keep their secret more secure. But for all their preparations, their long hours of planning and strategies, they could now only wait and see what the future held for them all.

The bookcase swings open to reveal the entryway to the secret annex.

9

Complications

By the fall of 1942, Anne and her family had been in hiding for several months. They were still safe, even if they never felt very secure.

Although they were isolated from the outside world, they were not entirely sealed off. They knew what was going on beyond the walls of the annex. News came to them from their friends, the helpers, as well as radio reports from the BBC that they would listen to each night.

Naturally, their biggest interest was in the progress of the war. How was it going? Were the Germans still winning? There was no simple answer to that question because

---

what is the BBC? The British Broadcasting Corporation. Its broadcasts from London provided news to people in the occupied countries.

the news seemed to go both ways. It was true that the Germans were no longer just rolling through countries and piling up new territory at will. Their forces, as well as those of their Japanese and Italian partners, were now meeting with resistance on every front. Their confidence was no longer so assured. Battles were being won by both sides. However, when the British and American forces landed in North Africa, many people jumped to the conclusion that this was the beginning of the end.

DID YOU KNOW?

Germany, Italy, and Japan were known as the Axis powers. The countries that opposed them were known as the Allies.

While some people thought the war was coming to a close, Anne, on the other hand, was feeling a bit more cautious. In her diary, she quoted the British prime minister, Winston Churchill. In a speech given on November 10, 1942, he had declared, "This is not the end. It is not even the beginning of the end. But it is, perhaps, the end of the beginning." She then added her own commentary to the quote: "Do you see the difference?"

THE PRIME MINISTER

Winston Churchill became the prime minister of Great Britain in 1940. He was a strong leader who gave inspiring speeches that people listened to around the world. Churchill had long opposed the Nazis during their rise to power in the 1930s, but the British government ignored his warnings until it was too late.

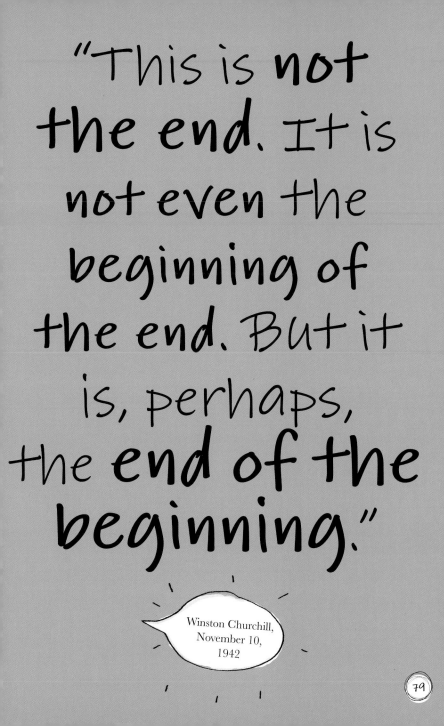

"This is **not** the end. It is not even the beginning of the end. But it is, perhaps, **the end of the beginning.**"

Winston Churchill, November 10, 1942

Jews wait in line to board a deportation train in the Netherlands.

In the Netherlands, the German grip on the population had tightened even more. The deportation of Jews was being stepped up with a ruthless efficiency. Every day new prisoners were plucked from their homes, from their businesses, or even from the streets as they walked. There was nowhere to run, and nowhere to hide.

Inside the annex, there was also no room for anyone to hide from one another. Tempers now flared easily, and patience was in short supply. If there had ever been any sense of adventure or excitement about living in the secret annex, it had completely worn off. As Anne wrote in late September 1942, "not being able to go outside upsets me more than I can say, and I'm terrified our hiding place will be discovered and that we'll be shot. That, of course, is a fairly dismal prospect."

---

what is deportation?   The process of forcibly taking people from their homes and sending them somewhere else to live.

Fritz Pfeffer

In November, a new refugee arrived in the annex. Fritz Pfeffer was a dentist known to both the Franks and the van Pelses. His situation was as desperate as theirs had been, and so they took him in. "If we can save even one of our friends," Otto reminded Anne, "the rest doesn't matter."

"The rest," as Otto put it, meant the new inconveniences that were now cropping up. The annex was getting more than a little crowded. Dr. Pfeffer's presence prompted some further room reshuffling. Margot began sleeping in her parents' room, leaving Anne to share her room with Dr. Pfeffer.

Anne patiently explained to Dr. Pfeffer about the daily

schedule and how quiet they had to be, but he seemed a bit surprised by all the restrictions. That surprised Anne in turn; they were, after all, living right under the noses of the police, as well as German collaborators and a great many people who simply would do whatever they were told. Anne couldn't help wondering what kind of life in hiding Dr. Pfeffer had been expecting instead.

The situation between Anne and Dr. Pfeffer did not improve over time. Before long she was complaining that Dr. Pfeffer, who had a reputation for being good with children and fond of them as well, "has turned out to be an old-fashioned disciplinarian and preacher of unbearably long sermons."

what is a German collaborator? In the Netherlands, someone who was Dutch by birth but agreed with Germany and was willing to help them.

These hardships were bearable, though, compared to the fate of the remaining Jews in the country. Anne had heard tales of the camp at Westerbork, in the northeast part of the Netherlands. She wrote down the rumors she had heard in her diary: "The people get almost nothing to eat, much less to drink, as water is available only one hour a day, and there's only one toilet and sink for several thousand people."

THE TRANSIT CAMP

Westerbork was the first stop for Jews the Germans had detained in the Netherlands. There the prisoners would be assessed for their skills and usefulness, divided into groups, then deported to their final destinations—the death camps.

At night, when Anne could more safely look out the window, she often saw German soldiers leading what she described as "long lines of good, innocent people" down the street. "No one is spared," she wrote in her diary. "The sick, the elderly, children, babies and pregnant women—all are marched to their death."

Such things were hard for Anne to accept—not just because they were so awful, but also because there was nothing she could do about them.

10

Keeping **hope** alive

As much as everyone in the annex focused on simply getting through one day at a time, thoughts would sometimes wander toward the future.

Anne and Margot still daydreamed about the lives they would lead after they were free again. Anne wanted to write. Margot was interested in some kind of nursing. But Anne found it

hard to concentrate while feeling like she was always being watched and judged by the grown-ups in the annex. "They criticize everything, and I mean everything, about me," she wrote, "my behavior, my personality, my manners; every inch of me, from head to toe and back again."

The others sometimes showed their nerves, too. One night in March 1943, Mrs. van Pels thought she heard thieves in the attic. Mr. van Pels could not imagine that anyone had broken in, but still he went to take a look. He did find thieves in a way—a few rats making off with some food. After that, the van Pels family cat, Mouschi, who they had brought with them, slept in the attic, and the rats kept their distance.

Larger battles were still being fought throughout Europe. Almost every night Anne could hear German planes flying overhead as they headed off on another mission. She hated that sound more than anything.

Anne may have heard this type of German fighter plane.

Despite the many dangers, the months continued to pass. Over the winter of 1944, Anne could feel herself truly growing up. She regretted some of her earlier childish outbursts, and she grew closer to Peter. He was still quiet, but they found more things to talk about—especially up in the attic, the only place where they could have some privacy.

Anne had always generally been interested in writing, but by this time, she had decided to become a journalist. It seemed like a natural fit. "And if I don't have the talent to write books or newspaper articles," Anne wrote in her diary, "I can always write for myself. But I want to achieve more than that."

DID YOU KNOW?

In April 1944, Anne and Peter shared a first kiss. The romance did not last long, but it was another step in making Anne feel she was growing up.

What is a journalist?

In Anne's time, someone who worked for a newspaper, magazine, or radio station, investigating and reporting about the news.

She could not see herself following her mother's example of staying home with her children. She wrote, "I need to have something besides a husband and children to devote myself to . . ."

It was that same month, in April 1944, that a burglary in the building made everyone more than a little nervous. The robbery itself didn't bother them anywhere near as much as the police coming to investigate. All eight inhabitants of the annex held their breaths, fearful that their pounding hearts would give them away, while the detectives investigated below.

Allied soldiers arrive on the shores of Normandy, France, on June 6, 1944.

A13-13

Fortunately, all was well. The police did not discover the people hiding in the annex. They remained safe for the moment.

Everyone continued to listen to the news on the radio, and they heard the war take a dramatic turn on June 6, 1944, when the Allied forces invaded Normandy, France. This began a push that would lead back into Germany itself.

Despite the positive news, the burglary episode stayed fresh in everyone's minds; it was a constant reminder that their freedom was never guaranteed, that it was always hanging by a thread.

Then one day, the thread broke.

On the morning of August 4, 1944, three

Dutch policemen and a German officer arrived at Prinsengracht 263. They had not come because of a burglary or to investigate a vague suspicion or rumor. No amount of protesting could turn them away.

They knew exactly where they were going, and what they would do once they got there.

They marched through the door and right into the office.

"Who is in charge here?" they asked Victor Kugler at gunpoint.

"I am," he replied.

They then asked to be shown the storeroom. A moment later one of the policeman swung open the bookcase door. Clearly he already knew what was behind it.

Up in the annex, the Franks, the van Pelses, and Dr. Pfeffer were quickly rounded up. There was nothing they could do, no way to resist. They were given a few minutes to gather their possessions, and then they were taken away.

The policemen trashed the annex looking for valuables. Anne's diary was left behind in scattered pages on the floor. Later Miep Gies carefully picked up the pages and saved them in her desk drawer, hoping to give them back to Anne when she returned.

How was the secret hiding place discovered? Who had tipped off the authorities? No one

knew for sure, and it remains something of a
mystery. It may have been one person, perhaps
someone who worked in the warehouse, or it
may have been simply a number of clues
collected over time.

For the Franks and the others, how they had
been found out didn't really matter. Their only
concern was what would happen next.

Time runs out

After the police's arrival at the annex, everything happened very fast.

The prisoners spent one night in a German security office where they were asked many questions. How long had they been hidden? Who had been helping them? The Franks could protect only some of their friends, because it was already obvious that anyone in charge of Otto's business would have had to have been involved. The Franks' friends and helpers were also questioned. Two of them, Johannes Kleiman and Victor Kugler, were arrested and imprisoned for a time. They refused to answer the police's questions.

The next day the Franks, the van Pelses, and Dr. Pfeffer were moved to a prison, and two days later they were moved again, this time to the Westerbork transit camp. Their time there was fairly short. A few weeks later they boarded a train for Poland and the concentration camp at Auschwitz.

The journey itself was a trial. There was no room to sit, no way to keep clean, and almost nothing to eat. Anne no longer had a diary to record her thoughts, but as she and the other prisoners were crammed onto freight cars, it is not hard to imagine her despair.

BREAKING BATTERIES

While they were in Westerbork, Anne and Margot had the job of breaking apart old batteries and separating the pieces into different barrels. This was a common task at the camps, and it was difficult work.

Railroad tracks lead to the camp's entry gates.

Once they arrived at Auschwitz, the prisoners were divided into two groups. Anyone who was thought to be too weak to work, which was mostly the older people and very young children, was immediately condemned to death. The rest of the prisoners, those who seemed to be strong and healthy enough, continued on for further inspection.

Anne feared that her father, who was not a particularly big or powerful-looking man, might have then been doomed. She couldn't know his fate for sure, though, because the men and women had been separated from one another.

Anne, Margot, and their mother were inspected and judged healthy enough to be useful. They were then forced to wait in long lines with the other female prisoners while numbered tattoos were etched onto their arms with a sharp pen. Their heads were shaved and they were given old, dirty clothes to change into.

By now it was clear that the Germans were losing the war. As the Russians began to advance on Poland from the east, the Germans decided to remove some prisoners from Auschwitz—but only those who were considered fit enough to still be useful. This time, Edith Frank did not pass the test. However, Anne and Margot, after being inspected again, this time under a harsh spotlight, were deemed strong enough to go.

NUMBERED TATTOOS

After the war was over, the numbers that were etched into the prisoners' arms at Auschwitz remained a symbol of the horror they endured.

Bergen-Belsen

Westerbork

POLAND

GERMANY

Auschwitz

Now separated from both their parents, the
sisters were transferred to the Bergen-Belsen
concentration camp near Hanover, Germany.
The conditions there were unspeakably bad.
Everything was dirty and unsanitary. Meals
were so meager that all the prisoners were
quickly reduced to nothing more than skin
and bones.

Anne and many others also developed
very uncomfortable skin infections, but the

greater risk came from their food and water. These were quickly contaminated with bacteria, which spread terrible diseases such as typhoid fever and dysentery.

Still, the prisoners managed to find a small bit of distraction by celebrating the holiday season. As one prisoner, Janny Brandes-Brilleslijper, later recalled, "We had saved up some stale bread and cut that into tiny pieces on which we spread onion and boiled cabbage. Our 'feast' nearly made us forget our misery for a few hours."

In the new year, Margot became so sick that she could no longer get out of bed. It was remembered later that Anne cared for her sister before becoming sick as well. Eventually Anne's clothes became so infected with lice and fleas that she had to throw them away and wrap herself in a blanket instead.

Meanwhile, the Allied forces were racing across Europe from the west. It was no longer a question of if the Germans would at last be defeated. It was only a question of when.

Sadly, this question was never answered for Anne. Like so many other prisoners in the camps, she was unable to survive the many months of brutal treatment. It was not just that she was ill. It was that her illness was ignored. Beyond a need for medicine, even a little more warmth or food might have made all the difference—but Anne had none of those things to comfort her.

First Margot, and then Anne, died of typhus, an infectious disease that had spread over their bodies and overcame them at last. Although the exact dates were not recorded, both Margot and Anne died in the late winter of 1945.

A few weeks later, on April 15, the Allies liberated, or freed, Bergen-Belsen. They found a camp filled with dead bodies and dying prisoners. Identifying the survivors was a grim task. Many could no longer walk. Others could barely speak. Even a smile required a greater effort than some could manage. For those who had held on that long, though, hope at least remained for the future.

Today, the sites of the camps serve as memorials to the people who suffered there.

THE legacy lives on

**The war in Europe finally ended when
the Germans surrendered on May 7, 1945.**

Of the eight people who had lived in the secret
annex, seven did not live to see that day. Besides
Anne and Margot, their mother, Edith, had
died in Auschwitz two months before the camp
was liberated. The three van Pelses had also
died. Dr. Pfeffer ended up in the Neuengamme
concentration camp near Hamburg, where he
died in December 1944.

TERRIBLE TRAGEDY

More than 70 percent of the Netherlands' Jewish population
did not survive World War II. In all, the Nazis murdered
nearly six million Jews across Europe. This horrific event
is now known as the Holocaust.

Only Otto Frank survived. Despite Anne's fears when he had been separated from the family, he was among those rescued from the Auschwitz concentration camp. As the war was ending, the German guards had been ordered to shoot the remaining prisoners before they left. They ran out of time before completing this task, and Otto was spared. He returned to Amsterdam where family friends slowly nursed him back to health.

For some time, Otto remained hopeful that Anne and Margot were still alive. Only when he met Janny Brandes-Brilleslijper, who had been in Bergen-Belsen when the two girls had died, did he finally learn the truth and give up hope.

Miep Gies gave Anne's diary to Otto upon his return to Amsterdam. While he was recuperating, Otto had the chance to read the diary for the first time. It was too

DID YOU KNOW?

Two pages Anne had tried to cover up because they were too personal were discovered in 2018.

painful for him to read it all at once, so he limited himself to a few pages a day. He was amazed by how clearly Anne had captured the life they had led in hiding as well as her own revelations about being a teenage girl.

Anne could be brutally honest when she wrote about the other inhabitants of the annex. At times her honesty pained Otto to read, but it was that same honesty that made her words all the more powerful.

There was another quality to Anne's writing that Otto noticed: Her thoughts and observations often went well beyond what one might expect of a person her age. "I see the world being slowly transformed into a wilderness," Anne had written. "I hear the approaching thunder that, one day, will destroy us too, I feel the suffering of millions. And yet, when I look up at the sky, I somehow feel that everything will change for the better, that this cruelty too shall end, that peace and tranquility will return once more."

Otto wanted to have Anne's diary published, but at first he found no interest from publishers. They thought people were tired of tragedies and wanted to put the grim memories of the war behind them. When Anne's diary became the subject of a newspaper article, though, it sparked some new interest.

The diary was first published in 1947, but its Dutch publisher was not hopeful about the sales prospects of *Het Achterhuis (The Secret Annex)*, as the book was first called. The first edition was limited to 1,500 copies. However, the publisher had severely underestimated the book's appeal.

THE ARTICLE

Dutch historian Jan Romein believed Anne's diary deserved to be published, so he wrote an article about it. The article, called *Kinderstem* ("A Child's Voice"), appeared on the front page of the newspaper *Het Parool* on April 3, 1946.

Anne's diary has been translated into more than
70 languages and published around the world.

Sales continued to grow, and the book has
remained in print ever since. The diary has also
been published in dozens of languages, as well
as adapted into a play and movie. "I want to go
on living even after my death!" Anne had
written just a few months before they were
captured. "And that's why I'm so grateful to
God for having given me this gift, which I can
use to develop myself and to express all that's
inside me!"

Anne herself had questioned whether she would ever write "something great." She did not live to see her fame become a reality, but she may have been pleased to know that her story has done more than just survive. Her words and her spirit have inspired many others who have appreciated the chance to get to know young Anne Frank.

Anne's
family tree

Michael Frank
1851–1909

Alice Betty
Frank
1865–1953

Robert
Frank
1886–1953

Uncle

Helene
Frank Elias
1893–1986

Aunt

Herbert
Frank
1891–1987

Uncle

Otto
Frank
1889–1980

Father

Margot also kept
a diary during
the war, but it
was never found.

Margot Betti
Frank
1926–1945

Sister

Grandfather

Abraham Holländer
1860–1927

Rosa Stern
Holländer
1866–1942

Grandmother

Mother

Edith
Holländer
Frank
1900–1945

Julius
Holländer
1894–1967

Walter
Holländer
1897–1968

Betti
Holländer
1898–1914

Uncle

Uncle

Aunt

Annelies
Marie Frank
1929–1945

Timeline

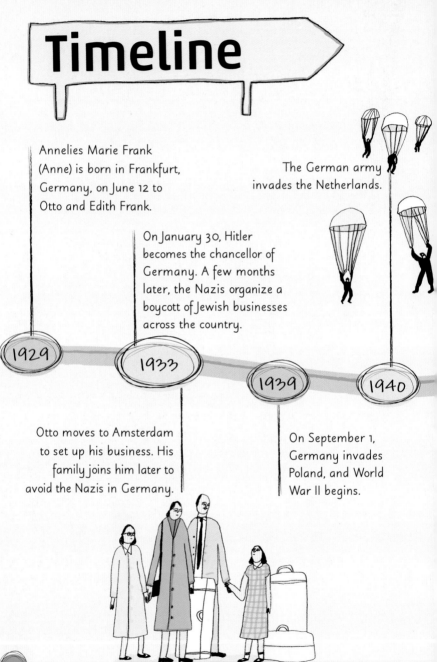

Annelies Marie Frank (Anne) is born in Frankfurt, Germany, on June 12 to Otto and Edith Frank.

On January 30, Hitler becomes the chancellor of Germany. A few months later, the Nazis organize a boycott of Jewish businesses across the country.

The German army invades the Netherlands.

1929

1933

1939

1940

Otto moves to Amsterdam to set up his business. His family joins him later to avoid the Nazis in Germany.

On September 1, Germany invades Poland, and World War II begins.

On July 5, Margot receives a summons ordering her to go to a labor camp. The Frank family goes into hiding the next day.

On July 13, the van Pels join the Franks in the secret annex.

1942

In November, Dr. Fritz Pfeffer becomes the final person to join the others in the annex.

On June 12, Anne receives a diary for her 13th birthday.

On June 6, the Allied forces land in Normandy, France, to free the country from German control.

In August, the residents of the secret annex are found and arrested. They are moved to the Westerbork transit camp.

1944

A few weeks later, the eight prisoners are transported to the Auschwitz concentration camp, where the men are separated from the women.

GERMANY

POLAND

Westerbork

Auschwitz

In late winter, Margot and Anne die within days of each other at the Bergen-Belsen concentration camp.

On January 6, Anne's mother, Edith, dies.

In July, Otto Frank learns about the death of his daughters. Miep Gies gives Anne's diary to Otto.

1945

1947

On January 27, the Russian army liberates the prisoners at Auschwitz— including Otto Frank.

On June 25, Anne's diary is published for the first time, in the Netherlands.

In June, Otto Frank makes his way back to Amsterdam after the war ends in Europe.

Quiz

1. In which year was Anne Frank born?

2. On which date did Adolf Hitler become the chancellor of Germany?

3. What pictures did Anne like to pin to her bedroom walls?

4. What does the German word *Kristallnacht* mean in English?

5. How many postcards did Anne tell her pen pal, Juanita, she had collected?

6. How were Jews forced to identify themselves in the streets?

7. Who from Anne's family was summoned to report to a labor camp on July 5, 1942?

Do you remember what you've read?
How many of these questions about
Anne's life can you answer?

8   How old was Peter van Pels when he went into hiding?

9   Which British prime minister did Anne quote in her diary?

10   Who collected the pages of Anne's diary after the secret annex was discovered?

11   In which concentration camp did Anne and Margot die in 1945?

12   Into how many languages has Anne's diary been translated?

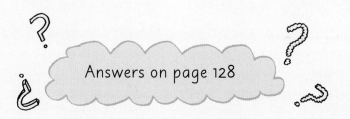

Answers on page 128

Who's who?

Brandes-Brilleslijper, Janny
(1916–2003) Dutch Holocaust survivor who was one of the last people to see Anne alive

Churchill, Winston
(1874–1965) prime minister of the United Kingdom from 1940 to 1945 and from 1951 to 1955. As prime minister, he led Britain to victory in World War II

Frank, Edith
(1900–1945) Anne's mother

Frank, Herbert
(1891–1987) Anne's uncle who she called "Uncle Blue Dot"; her father's younger brother

Frank, Margot
(1926–1945) Anne's older sister

Frank, Otto
(1889–1980) Anne's father; only resident of the secret annex who survived the Holocaust; arranged for the publication of Anne's diary after the war

Gies, Hermine ("Miep")
(1909–2010) one of Otto's employees and close friends; helped the Franks while they were in hiding

Hitler, Adolf
(1889–1945) leader of the Nazi Party; chancellor of Germany from 1933 to 1945

Holländer, Rose Stern
(1866–1942) Anne's grandmother on her mother's side, who she lived with for a few months before moving to Amsterdam

Kleiman, Johannes
(1896–1959) bookkeeper for Otto's companies; helped the Franks while they were in hiding

Kugler, Victor
(1900–1981) one of Otto's business partners; helped

the Franks while they were in hiding

Pfeffer, Friedrich ("Fritz")
(1889–1944) German dentist who hid with the Franks and van Pelses in the secret annex

Princess Elizabeth
(1926–) current queen of the United Kingdom. Elizabeth was a princess during World War II and one of Anne's favorite royals

Princess Juliana
(1909–2004) queen of the Netherlands from 1948 to 1980. Juliana was a princess during World War II and one of Anne's favorite royals

Princess Margaret
(1930–2002) younger sister of Queen Elizabeth of the United Kingdom. Margaret was a princess during World War II and one of Anne's favorite royals

Queen Wilhelmina
(1880–1962) queen of the Netherlands during World

War II; one of Anne's favorite royals

van Pels, Auguste ("Gusti")
(1900–1945) resident of the secret annex; Gusti and her family joined the Franks a week after they had moved into the secret annex

van Pels, Hermann
(1898–1944) colleague of Otto's; one of the residents in the secret annex

van Pels, Peter
(1926–1945) only child of Gusti and Hermann van Pels; one of the residents of the secret annex

Voskuijl, Elizabeth ("Bep")
(1919–1983) one of Otto's employees; helped the Franks while they were in hiding

Voskuijl, Johannes Hendrik
(1892–1945) Bep's father; designed and built the bookcase that hid the entrance to the annex

Glossary

annex
rooms that are an extension to a main building

Anschluss
merging of Germany and Austria in 1938

anti-Semitism
hatred of all things Jewish, including Jews themselves

BBC
British Broadcasting Corporation—a British organization that airs programs on television and radio

boycott
form of protest in which someone refuses to deal with a certain person or organization

colic
condition that can cause babies to cry for more than three hours without stopping

concentration camps
confined areas set up by the Nazis in which Jews and other people were imprisoned and treated in inhumane ways

Czechoslovakia
former European country now divided into the Czech Republic and Slovakia

deportation
act of forcibly sending people away, either to

another country to live
or to a prison

disciplinarian
someone who is
very strict

dislocate
pull bones out of
their normal position
in a joint

dysentery
serious infection that
causes fever, abdominal
pain, and diarrhea

emigration
act of people moving
permanently from one
country to another

exile
living outside your
own country, usually
not by choice

freight car
railroad car that
transports goods

**German
colloborator**
non-German person
who agreed with the
Nazis during Word
War II and was willing
to help them

governess
woman hired to teach
children at home

Holocaust
period from 1933 to
1945 during which the
Nazis planned and
carried out the murder
of six million Jews

inflation
increase in prices
that occurs naturally
over time

Jew
person whose religion,
or family religion, is
Judaism

journalist
reporter for a
newspaper, magazine,
or radio station

Kristallnacht
"Night of Broken Glass";
wave of violence toward
Jews and their businesses
and homes in Germany
on November 9, 1938

labor camp
prison in which the
inmates are forced to
do hard, physical work

lice
wingless insects that suck
blood and may spread
diseases; singular: louse

lyceum
type of school

mimicry
copying, or
impersonating, another
person or animal

Nazi
member of the
Nationalist-Socialist
German Workers' Party,
which took control of
Germany in 1933

ominously
suggesting that
something bad is
going to happen

pen pals
two people who write
letters back and forth
to each other

revelation
previously unknown
fact, often surprising

Rhineland
area in western
Germany occupied
by foreign powers in
the years before
World War II

summons
official request or
command to appear at
a specific place, usually
at a chosen time

transit camp
temporary camp where
prisoners are assessed
for their usefulness
before being moved
on to other camps

typhoid fever
infection that can cause
fever, rash, and diarrhea

typhus
deadly disease carried
by lice

whooping cough
illness, usually affecting
children, with a
distinctive cough

Index

125